DEGAS *Women Ironing*

Between Here and Now

R. S. Thomas

M

ISBN 0 333 32186 3 (hardcover)
ISBN 0 333 32629 6 (paperback)

First published 1981 by
Macmillan London Limited
London and Basingstoke

Associated companies in Auckland, Dallas,
Delhi, Dublin, Hong Kong, Johannesburg,
Lagos, Manzini, Melbourne, Nairobi,
New York, Singapore, Tokyo, Washington
and Zaria

Printed in Great Britain by
Butler & Tanner Ltd
Frome and London

For Marie-Thérèse Castay

CONTENTS

7

OTHER POEMS

IMPRESSIONS

With acknowledgments to *Impressionist Paintings in the Louvre*
by Germain Bazin (Thames and Hudson, 1958)

MONET *Lady with a Parasol*

Why keep the sun
from the head, when the grass
is a fire about
the feet? She wields her umbrella

from fashion, a not
too serious shield against
summer's unreal missiles. She
is brown already. What

she carries is a pretence
at effeminacy, a borrowing
from the mystery shadow
concocts. But that arm

is sturdy, the carriage
erect, the bust ample enough
for a peasant to lay his
head there, dreaming of harvest.

Harbour, Havre 63 Long Reed

An agreement between
land and sea, with both using
the same tone? But the boat,
motionless in the sand, refuses

to endorse it, remembering
the fury of the clawing
of white hands. However skilfully
the blue surface mirrors

the sky, to the boat it is
the glass lid of a coffin
within which by cold lips
the wooden carcases are mumbled.

MONET *The Bas-Bréau Road*

Who bothers
        where this road goes?
It is not for getting people
        anywhere, at least
not at speed. It found a gap
in the forest and dawdles
        like a slow river,
looking-glass smooth, letting
        the leaves fall on it,
not carrying them off.

It has the quietness of time
        before the first motor-car
startled it, worrying it
with such ideas as
        that there are destinations.

BAZILLE *Family Reunion*

In groups
        under the tree,
none of them sorry
for having partaken
            of its knowledge.

Sex? They wanted
        it. Children?
Why not?
        And clothes, clothes:
        how they outdo
            their background.

Their looks challenge
        us to find
            where they failed.

Well-dressed, well-
fed; their servants
        are out of sight,
snatching a moment
            to beget offspring
who are to overturn all this.

DEGAS *Portrait of a Young Woman*

I imagine he intended
other things: tonal
values, the light and shade
of her cheek.
                  To me innocence
is its meaning. If the lips
opened a little, blessings
would come forth. Those eyes
have looked upon evil
and not seen it. Her young being
waits to be startled
by the sweetness in roughness
of hands that
with permitted boldness
will remove her bark
to show under how smooth a
tree temptation can shelter.

MONET *Portrait of Madame Gaudibert*

Waiting for the curtain
to rise on an audience
        of one – her husband
who, knowledgeable about ships,
knew how to salvage
        the ship-wrecked painter.

        Comforting
to think how, for a moment
at least, Monet on even
keel paddled himself
on with strokes not
                        of an oar but
        of a fast-dipping brush.

DEGAS *Mademoiselle Dihau at the Piano*

Asking us what she shall play?
    But she is her own
music, calm rather than
    sad, mahogany-
toned. We listen to her
    as, on an afternoon
in September, the garden listens
    to the year ripening. Almost
we could reach out a hand
    for the mellow-fleshed,
sun-polished fruit
    that she is. But her eyes
are the seeds of a tart
    apple, and the score a notice
against trespassing upon
    land so privately owned.

DEGAS *Musicians in the Orchestra*

Heads together, pulling
　　　upon music's tide –
it is not their ears
　　　but their eyes their conductor

has sealed, lest they behold
　　　on the stage's shore
the skirts' rising and falling
　　　that turns men to swine.

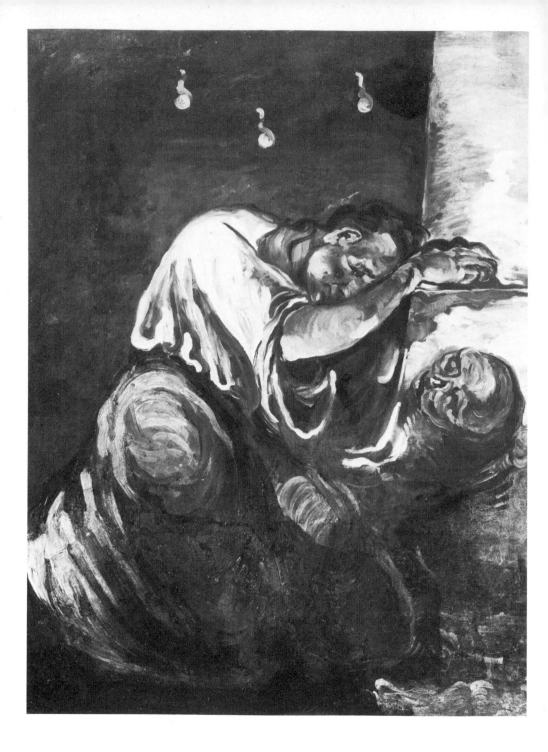

CÉZANNE *The Repentant Magdalen*

So three tears are enough,
    a little water
to clear the flesh of
    its offences. She loved
much, so is free
    of remorse. Daughters
of Jerusalem – but where
    are they? The tears
are three hooks to hang
    the other sacrifices
from. What she repents of
    is no matter. Mankind's
place beside the crucified
    God is upon
its knees. The harlot anticipates
    sophisticated minds. The painter
standing aside has shown
    us eternity's rainbow
after the human storm.

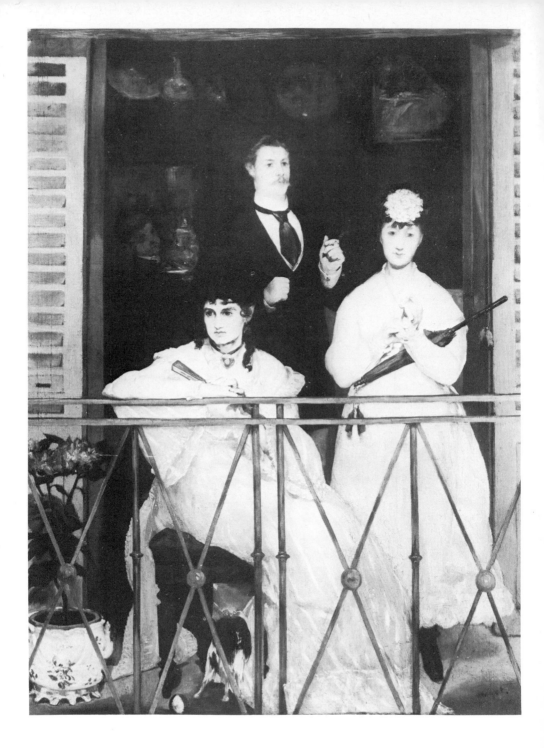

MANET *The Balcony*

We watch them. They watch
what? The world passes,
they remain, looking
as they were meant to do

at a spectacle
beyond us. It affects them
in several ways. One stares
as at her fortune

being told. One's hands
are together as if
in applause. The monsieur surmounts
them in sartorial calm.

CÉZANNE *Dr Gachet's House*

Wanting to find out
if it was on the edge
of something? But the surroundings
blurred; only the way to it

clear, as it was meant
to be for the earless painter
coming with his mind in pieces
to mend it by the light of those eyes.

35

DEGAS *The Dancing Class*

Pretending he keeps
an aviary; looking no higher
than their feet; listening
for their precise fluttering.

And they surround him, flightless
birds in taffeta
plumage, picking up words
gratefully, as though they were crumbs.

MONET *The Gare Saint-Lazare*

The engines
    are ready to start,
but why travel
    where they are aimed
at?
    What skies as indigo
as their coughed smoke?
    The passengers appear
to attest this, lingering
    on, syringing their ears
with escaping steam
    of the old sounds from the fields
that have accumulated there
    over the centuries like wax.

PISSARRO *Kitchen Garden, Trees in Bloom*

I know this house,
    though there are few such
on rising ground
    over a plumed orchard.

I know the dry smell
    of sunlight in rooms
where the clock's insect
    aggravates the hour.

Art is recuperation
    from time. I lie back
convalescing upon the prospect
    of a harvest already at hand.

DEGAS *Absinthe*

She didn't want to go;
she couldn't resist.
It was an opportunity
to be like other women,

to sit at an inn table,
not drinking, but repenting
for having drunk of a liquid
that made such promises

as it could not fulfil.
Her clothes are out of the top
drawer, the best her class
could provide. The presence

of the swarthier ruffian
beside her guarantees
that she put them on in order
to have something good she could take off.

PISSARRO *Landscape at Chaponval*

It would be good to live
in this village with time
stationary and the clouds
going by. The grass is a tide

rising and falling. The cow
sips it. The woman stands
patiently by the slow udder
as at a cistern filling.

RENOIR   *Muslim Festival at Algiers*

People: their combs and wattles
rampant upon a background
of dung. The dancers silently
crackling on an unquenched hearth.

A mosque, a tower as deputies
in the clouds' absence; and gazing,
as at a window, the detached
ocean with its cerulean stare.

Has a bridge
to be crossed? Better empty
this one, awaiting
the traveller's return

from the outside
world to his place
at the handrail to
watch for the face's

water-lily to emerge
from the dark depths
as quietly as the waxen
moon from among clouds.

CÉZANNE   *The Card Players*

And neither of them has said:
        Your lead.
                An absence of trumps
will arrest movement.

        Knees almost touching,
        hands almost touching,
                they are far away
in time in a world
                of equations.

                The pipe without
        smoke, the empty
        bottle, the light
on the wall are the clock
        they go by.
                Only their minds
                lazily as flies
                        drift
round and round the inane
problem their boredom
                has led them to pose.

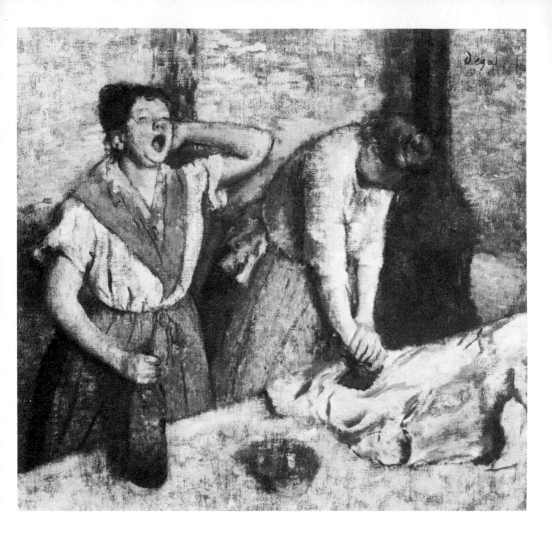

DEGAS *Women Ironing*

one hand
    on cheek the other
on the bottle
    mouth open
her neighbour
    with hands clasped
not in prayer
    her head bent
over her decreasing
    function   this is art
overcoming permanently
    the temptation to answer
a yawn with a yawn

CASSATT   *Young Woman Sewing*

Sewing. Is she one
of the three fates, the first,
perhaps, presiding over
a far birth, her fingers

as though they would join together
what her brows parted? She is
the chrysalis she
inhabits, but the blood

in flower about her
is an indication of the arrival
of her period to come
out now and spread her wings.

GAUGUIN *Breton Landscape, the Mill*

The eye is to concentrate
on the tree gushing
over the bent-backed woman
with her companion and
dog. But there is so much
besides: the wheel too heavy
to be turned by such still
water; the hill-side; the house
asleep in its counterpane
of colour; and beyond
them all the whey-faced cloud
agog as at a far sill.

GAUGUIN *The Alyscamps at Arles*

Shining morning!
A trinity of figures –
coming from Mass? They
have the stiffness of candles.

The century's convention
drew them inside; but out
here, pure as the sky,
is the living water, and the leaves

over them have the crispness
of bread. Art is a sacrament
in itself. Now that
the angelus is silent

the brush-strokes go on
calling from the canvas's
airier belfries
to the celebration of colour.

We know someone like this.
An imaginary circle
separates her from the blue
of the night, whose flowers
are moth-winged.

                      Beside her
in bronze is her other
self, the cat-like image
that causes her to sheathe
her fingers and try looking
as demure as the small
cross on her bosom tells
her she ought to be.

VAN GOGH   *Portrait of Dr Gachet*

Not part of the Health Service;
no-one to pass his failures
on to. The eyes like quinine
have the same medicative

power. With one hand
on cheek, the other
on the equivocal
foxglove he listens

to life as it describes
its symptoms, a doctor
becoming patient himself
of art's diagnosis.

VAN GOGH *The Church at Auvers*

So large a church
    for so small
a village, yet still
    not big enough
for the stupendous presence.
    It divides the path
as a rock
    in mid-stream.
                The
woman is not going
    there. Though Catholic
she is one of Herbert's
    people, who sweep
rooms, scrub floors,
    down on their knees
as the angelus rings
    out from an uncaring belfry.

TOULOUSE-LAUTREC   *Jane Avril Dancing*

Such daring!
    With the couple in the corner
looking at one another
for approval.

        All up to the neck
in their conventions;
              she only
    showing the knees
by which some would gain entrance to heaven.

TOULOUSE-LAUTREC *Justine Dieuhl*

As we would always wish
   to find her waiting for us,
seated, delphinium-eyed, dressed
for the occasion; out of doors
   since it is always warm
where she is.
           The red kerchief
at the neck, that suggests
blood, is art leading
   modesty astray.
           The hands,
large enough for encircling
the waist's stem, are,
   as ours should be, in
perfect repose, not accessory
to the plucking of her own flower.

GAUGUIN *Breton Village in the Snow*

This is the village
    to which the lost traveller
came, searching for his first spring,
    and found, lying asleep
in the young snow, how cold
    was its blossom.
                    The trees
are of iron, but nothing
    is forged on them. The tower
is a finger pointing
    up, but at whom?
                    If prayers
are said here, they are
    for a hand to roll
back this white quilt
    and uncover the bed
where the earth is asleep,
    too, but nearer awaking.

But deep inside
are the chipped figures
with their budgerigar faces,
a sort of divine
humour in collusion
with time. Who but
God can improve
by distortion?
        There is
a stone twittering in
the cathedral branches,
the excitement of migrants
newly arrived from a tremendous
presence.
        We have no food
for them but our
prayers. Kneeling we drop our
crumbs, apologising
for their dryness, afraid
to look up in the ensuing
silence in case they have flown.

ROUSSEAU *The Snake Charmer*

A bird not of this
planet; serpents earlier
than their venom; plants
reduplicating the moon's

paleness. An anonymous
minstrel, threatening us
from under macabre
boughs with the innocence

of his music. The dark
listens to him and withholds
till to-morrow the boneless
progeny to be brought to birth.

RENOIR   *The Bathers*

What do they say?
    Here is flesh
not to be peeped
    at. No Godivas
these. They remain
    not pass, naked
for us to gaze
    our fill on, but
without lust.
           This
    is the mind's feast,
where taste follows
    participation. Values
are in reverse
    here. Such soft tones
are for the eye
    only. These bodies,
smooth as bells
    from art's stroking, toll
an unheard music,
    keep such firmness
of line as never,
    under the lapping
of all this light
    to become blurred or dim.

OTHER POEMS

DIRECTIONS

In this desert of language
  we find ourselves in,
with the sign-post with the word 'God'
  worn away
     and the distance ... ?

Pity the simpleton
  with his mouth open crying:
     How far is it to God?

And the wiseacre says: Where you were,
friend.
  You know that smile
      glossy
as the machine that thinks it has outpaced
  belief?
    I am one of those
who sees from the arms opened
    to embrace the future
the shadow of the Cross fall
  on the smoothest of surfaces
    causing me to stumble.

COVENANT

I feel sometimes
    we are his penance
for having made us. He
suffers in us and we partake
    of his suffering. What
to do, when it has been done
    already? Where
    to go, when the arrival
is as the departure? Circularity
is a mental condition, the
animals know nothing of it.

    Seven times have passed
over him, and he is still here.
    When will he return
from his human exile, and will
peace then be restored
    to the flesh?
                Often
I think that there is no end
to this torment and that the electricity
that convulses us is the fire
    in which a god
burns and is not consumed.

WAITING

Yeats said that. Young
I delighted in it:
there was time enough.

Fingers burned, heart
seared, a bad taste
in the mouth, I read him

again, but without trust
any more. What counsel
has the pen's rhetoric

to impart? Break mirrors, stare
ghosts in the face, try
walking without crutches

at the grave's edge? Now
in the small hours
of belief the one eloquence

to master is that
of the bowed head, the bent
knee, waiting, as at the end

of a hard winter
for one flower to open
on the mind's tree of thorns.

SARABAND

That was before the Revolution
as it must always be for the heart
to appraise it. I think they met
in the peculiar sultriness
of August ... And the voice says: Carry
on; I am interested. But I labour
to find my way. It is true
that I made my choice and the poem
cannot hit back; but the colour of it
is not that which her eyes made,
cold stones in the fierce river
of his breath, while the lark's clockwork
went on and on.
             What a wild country
it is, as hot and dry for one part
of the year, as it is dead and cold
for the other; and the frost comes down
like a great bird, hovering silently
over the homes of an inert people
who have never known either freedom or love.

CORRESPONDENCE

You ask why I don't write.
But what is there to say?
The salt current swings in and out
of the bay, as it has done
time out of mind. How does that help?
It leaves illegible writing
on the shore. If you were here,
we would quarrel about it.
People file past this seascape
as ignorantly as through a gallery
of great art. I keep searching for meaning.
The waves are a moving staircase
to climb, but in thought only.
The fall from the top is as sheer
as ever. Younger I deemed truth
was to come at beyond the horizon.
Older I stay still and am
as far off as before. These nail-parings
bore you? They explain my silence.
I wish there were as simple
an explanation for the silence of God.

AIE!

The flowers of childhood
are fadeless and have
a sweet smell. Our hearts are
vases, standing in the window

· that looks out on to Eden's
garden. But our minds
are of glass also and
refrigerate us with a different view.

SKELETON

Smiling? An euphemism
for showing the teeth?
This one – three thousand years
dead – harmless? There is a secret
he teases us with, something
he keeps to himself: the knowledge
that man is a revolving
glass; that he in his day
focused the light as clearly
as we in ours; that for a moment
the darkness was less dark,
the interval was tenanted
by flowers and music, the dust, too,
had a serene halo.
               From beyond
his horizons the presence
he was somehow a part of
drew near with its implicit insistence
that the light is perennial,
that the flesh is a lens
continually re-ground; that somewhere
within the personal crystal
are memories of its anterior
shinings, a prophecy
of others endlessly to come.

EVENING

From his window he looked out
on a wood from which
flocks of birds, many
as his thoughts, periodically

would erupt. Below him
the wild swans of the sea
came drifting in to die
on the shore. There was no question

of why he was there; he
was there with a fire
of sticks and the words that
over a long life

should have appreciated
adequately to the purchase
of the things grown dearer
in the slow setting of his sun.

PLUPERFECT

It was because there was nothing to do
that I did it; because silence was golden
I broke it. There was a vacuum
I found myself in, full of echoes
of dead languages. Where to turn
when there are no corners? In curved
space I kept on arriving
at my departures. I left no stones
unraised, but always wings
were tardy to start. In ante-rooms
of the spirit I suffered the anaesthetic
of time and came to with my hurt
unmended. Where are you? I
shouted, growing old in
the interval between here and now.

FAIR DAY

They come in from the fields
with the dew and the buttercup dust
on their boots. It was not they
nor their ancestors crucified
Christ. They look up at what
the town has done to him,
hanging his body in stone on a stone
cross, as though to commemorate
the bringing of the divine beast
to bay and disabling him.

He is hung up high, but higher
are the cranes and scaffolding
of the future. And they stand by,
men from the past, whose rôle
is to assist in the destruction
of the past, bringing their own beasts
in to offer their blood up
on a shoddier altar.
                              The town
is malignant. It grows, and what
it feeds on is what these men call
their home. Is there praise
here? There is the noise of those
buying and selling and mortgaging
their conscience, while the stone
eyes look down tearlessly. There
is not even anger in them any more.

VOICES

Who to believe?
The linnet sings bell-like,
a tinkling music. It says life
is contained here; is a jewel

in a shell casket, lying
among down. There is another
voice, far out in space,
whose persuasiveness is the distance

from which it speaks. Divided
mind, the message is always
in two parts. Must it be
on a cross it is made one?

ARRIVING

A maze, he said,
    and at the centre
    the Minotaur
       awaits us.

There are turnings
    that are no through road
    to the fearful.
       By one I came

travelling it
    like a gallery
    of the imagination,
       pausing to look

at the invisible portraits
    of brave men.
    Their deeds rustled
       like dry leaves

under my tread.
    The scent of them was
    the dust we throw
       in the eyes of the beast.

ALEPH

What is time? The man stands
in the grass under
the willow by the grey
water corrugated
by wind, and his spirit reminds
him of how it was always
so, in Athens, in Sumer under
the great king. The moment
is history's navel
and round it the worlds
spin. Was there desire
in the past? It is fulfilled
here. The mind has emerged
from the long cave without
looking back, leading eternity
by the hand, and together they pause
on the adult threshold
recuperating endlessly
in intermissions of the machine.

CODE

He grew up into an emptiness
he was on terms with. The duplicity
of language, that could name
what was not there, was accepted

by him. He was content, remembering
the unseen writing of Christ
on the ground, to interpret
it in his own way. Adultery

of the flesh has the divine
pardon. It is the mind,
catching itself in the act
of unfaithfulness, that must cast no stone.

THE NEW MARINER

In the silence
that is his chosen medium
of communication and telling
others about it
in words. Is there no way
not to be the sport
of reason? For me now
there is only the God-space
into which I send out
my probes. I had looked forward
to old age as a time
of quietness, a time to draw
my horizons about me,
to watch memories ripening
in the sunlight of a walled garden.
But there is the void
over my head and the distance
within that the tireless signals
come from. And astronaut
on impossible journeys
to the far side of the self
I return with messages
I cannot decipher, garrulous
about them, worrying the ear
of the passer-by, hot on his way
to the marriage of plain fact with plain fact.

BEACONS

Whose address was the corridors
of Europe, waiting for the summons
to be interrogated on their lack of guilt.

Their flesh was dough for the hot
ovens. Some of them rose
to the occasion. The nerves of some

were instruments on which the guards fingered
obscene music. Were there prayers
said? Did a god hear? Time heard

them, anticipating their requital.
Their wrong is an echo defying
acoustical law, increasing not fading.

Evil's crumbling anonymity
is at an end now. We recognise
it by the eternal phosphorous

of their bones, and make our way on
by that same light to the birth
of an innocence that is curled up in the will.

FLAT

Yesterday a sinner,
today fetching my soul
from the divine laundry
to wear it in the march past
tomorrow of the multitude
of white robes no man
can number?
    Too simple.
There are girls, reversions,
the purse's incontinence.
Truth has its off-days,
too.
    Forgetting yesterday,
ignorant of the future,
I take up apartments
in the here and now, furnishing
them with my reflections,
renting them with each breath
I draw; staring from a window
without view in the spurious
silence of an electric clock.

BENT

Heads bowed
          over the entrails,
over the manuscript, the
block, over the rows
                    of swedes.

Do they never look up?
          Why should one think
that to be on one's knees
          is to pray?
The aim is to walk tall
                    in the sun.
Did the weight of the jaw
          bend their backs,
keeping their vision
          below the horizon?

Two million years
in straightening them
          out, and they are still bent
over the charts, the instruments,
                    the drawing-board,
the mathematical navel
          that is the wink of God.

FLOWERS

But behind the flower
is that other flower
which is ageless, the idea
of the flower, the one
we smell when we imagine
it, that as often
as it is picked blossoms
again, that has the perfection
of all flowers, the purity
without the fragility.
     Was it
a part of the plan
for humanity to have
flowers about it? They are many
and beautiful, with faces
that are a reminder of those
of our own children, though they come painlessly
from the bulb's womb. We trouble
them as we go by, so they hang
their heads at our unreal
progress.
    If flowers had minds,
would they not think they were the colour
eternity is, a window that gives
on a still view the hurrying
people must come to and stare at and pass by?

MINOR

Nietzsche had a word
for it. History discredits
his language. Ours
more quietly rusts

in autumnal libraries
of the spirit. Scolded
for small faults, we see
how violence in others

is secretly respected.
Do we amble pacifically
towards our extinction? The answers
from over the water

are blood-red. I wonder,
seeing the rock
split by green grass
as efficiently

as the atom, is this
the centre from which
nature will watch out
human folly, until

it is time to call back
to the small field civilisation
began in the small
people the giants deposed?

OBSERVATION

Recalling adventures:
One person, he thinks,
in every century or so
came within hail.
I answered by standing
aside, watching him
as he passed. I
am the eternal quarry,
moving at thought's
speed, following
the hunter, arriving
before him. They
put down their prayers'
bait, and swallow it
themselves. Somewhere
between word and deed
are the equations
I step over. Why
do they stare out
with appalled minds
at the appetite
of their lenses?
It is where I feed,
too, waiting for them
to catch up, bounded
only by an inability
to be overtaken.

PATTERNS

The old men ask
for more time, while the young
waste it. And the philosopher
smiles, knowing there is none

there. But the hero stands
sword drawn at the looking-glass
of his mind, aiming at that
anonymous face over his shoulder.

THE PRESENCE

I pray and incur
silence. Some take that silence
for refusal.
       I feel the power
that, invisible, catches me
by the sleeve, nudging
       towards the long shelf
that has the book on it I will take down
       and read and find the antidote
to an ailment.
       I know its ways with me;
how it enters my life,
       is present rather
before I perceive it, sunlight quivering
on a bare wall.
       Is it consciousness trying
to get through?
       Am I under
regard?
       It takes me seconds
to focus, by which time
       it has shifted its gaze,
looking a little to one
       side, as though I were not here.

It has the universe
       to be abroad in.
There is nothing I can do
but fill myself with my own
       silence, hoping it will approach
       like a wild creature to drink
there, or perhaps like Narcissus
to linger a moment over its transparent face.

FOREST DWELLERS

Men who have hardly uncurled
from their posture in the
womb. Naked. Heads bowed, not
in prayer, but in contemplation
of the earth they came from,
that suckled them on the brown
milk that builds bone not brain.

Who called them forth to walk
in the green light, their thoughts
on darkness? Their women,
who are not Madonnas, have babes
at the breast with the wise,
time-ridden faces of the Christ
child in a painting by a Florentine

master. The warriors prepare poison
with love's care for the Sebastians
of their arrows. They have no
God, but follow the contradictions
of a ritual that says
life must die that life
may go on. They wear flowers in their hair.

RETURN

Taking the next train
to the city, yet always returning
to his place on a bridge
over a river, throbbing

with trout, whose widening
circles are the mandala
for contentment. So will a poet
return to the work laid

on one side and abandoned
for the voices summoning him
to the wrong tasks. Art
is not life. It is not the river

carrying us away, but the motionless
image of itself on a fast-
running surface with which life
tries constantly to keep up.

THRESHOLD

I emerge from the mind's
cave into the worse darkness
outside, where things pass and
the Lord is in none of them.

I have heard the still, small voice
and it was that of the bacteria
demolishing my cosmos. I
have lingered too long on

this threshold, but where can I go?
To look back is to lose the soul
I was leading upward towards
the light. To look forward? Ah,

what balance is needed at
the edges of such an abyss.
I am alone on the surface
of a turning planet. What

to do but, like Michelangelo's
Adam, put my hand
out into unknown space,
hoping for the reciprocating touch?